THE POWER OF THE PIPS

THE POWER OF THE PIPS

courting numbers in cartomancy

CAMELIA ELIAS

EYECORNER PRESS

THE POWER OF THE PIPS:
COURTING NUMBERS IN CARTOMANCY

Published by EYECORNER PRESS
in the series **Divination Books**

February 2018, Thy, Denmark

ISBN: 978-87-92633-39-2

Cover design, image, and layout: Camelia Elias

Images of the Tarot:

Marseille Tarot by Jean Noblet, 1650
reconstructed by Jean-Claude Flornoy.

With kind permission by Roxanne Flornoy.

Printed in the UK and US

FOR BENT

Contents

SMALL SEDUCTIONS / 9

A SHORT THEORY OF THE PIP CARDS / 15

A SHORT THEORY OF THE COURT CARDS / 27

WISHING WELL / 53

HUMOR ME / 59

BELIEVABLE STORIES / 65

WAIT FOR IT / 79

THE DECISIVE FACTOR / 89

BURNING BRIDGES / 101

FREE WILL / 105

Small Seductions

When the series of eight lectures *The Power of the Trumps* was released last year (video and book form), it was received with great applause.

'This is not just about cards, this is about life and a lot more,' people said, gradually expressing what became a consensus opinion.

People are right. My work with the cards is not about cards for the sake of history, aesthetics, or even divination practices, but about 'life and more' simply because there's great attention that goes into figuring out how images on cardboard participate in expanding our field of habitual thinking beyond cultural dictations.

'This is not just about cards, this is about life and a lot more,' is thus a statement about what happens when we read cards in context, which is to say, when we anchor our interpretations in a specific question related to a specific situation.

But what can we say about reading the pip cards, the number cards devoid of figurative images representing people 'doing' life?

What do we do about all that geometry and gardening, judging by the arrangement of elements in our stylized suits, with coins, cups, batons, and swords crossing each other or running parallel, embellished also in their 'action' by vine leaves or other floral suggestions?

What about the ever-contradictory theories about the court cards as aspects of ourselves, archetypes, or as extensions of standard human behavior, ranging from embodiments of critics and abusers to healers and heroes?

Here comes *The Power of the Pips,* the companion book to *The Power of the Trumps.*

My theory is that the power of the minor arcana of the tarot is all about courting. Whether we like it or not, we're all seduced by the abstractness of numbers and by the desired identity that the court cards can offer us.

Who doesn't fancy herself as a mean Queen of Spades, if your practice has any occult leanings?

Who doesn't fancy himself as a man of cunning resource, sitting solidly on a whole bank, and affording the luxury of generosity? I have as yet to see a magician who thinks poverty is part of the practice. There are exceptions, of course, when the magician is a monk, but that's rare.

In this book we look at the ways in which the pip cards have a story to tell that's all their own.

As I've written before on the basic method of reading the pip cards in my book, *Marseille Tarot: Towards the Art of Reading* (2015), I will not repeat here what I said there.

Here I want to present you with a similar approach to reading cards in context as exhibited in my other, related book *The Power of the Trumps* (2016).

This means that there's a specific idea that guides my reading, either based on a concrete question, or one that springs from a troubling matter or concern.

The idea is to give you something to think about, while also giving you a specific model for how you can approach reading the pip cards.

My preferred method is to teach by example. If I have a theory, I give it to you in the form of an example.

Because we have two different types of cards that compose the so-called minor arcana of the Marseille Tarot, number cards and court cards, I will first introduce you briefly to the principles of strategy of reading the pip cards, and then offer as well an ampler discussion of what to make of the court cards. Both of these texts have circulated in some form or other on my blog, *Taroflexions,* and my column, *The Cartomancer* with Patheos.

In their revised and expanded form here, these texts will form the first part of this book, laying the ground for a more playful and spontaneous approach to the pip cards. This approach consists of reading strings of three cards or more as they connect to what we often encounter in life situations, whether of mundane or more metaphysical character.

In terms of style, you can expect to see here the same approach to cartomancy that I also like to associate with the idea of martial arts, or going for the clean cut. This is another way of saying that I read the cards like the Devil, aiming for penetrating insight.

This is a stringent approach to the spontaneous, in the sense that what I have to offer is very much anchored in deconstructing Zen style language, clichés, mainstream opinions, and other 'natural' approaches to thinking. My sole aim is to make you go: 'Why didn't I think of this before?'

Knowing all your cards, trumps, pips, and courts, is knowing how to string together a narrative that makes sense and is useful. In other words, knowing your cards is knowing what makes you a good diviner; a diviner that's not invested in borrowed lists of meanings, comparison, fear of inadequacy, or strategies of compensating for the lack of personal nerve and original voice.

What makes a good diviner is this: Knowing that the cards are a perfect mirror. A perfect mirror is not truth. People come to ask a question. You don't 'help' them. You let the mirror reflect the deep and hidden answers. You are reliable in your practice. You say: 'This is your story. It ends like this.'

Enjoy the ride with the power of the pip cards, all about courting you and your skills in seeing the obvious.

A Short Theory of the Pip Cards

In our work with the cards, we talk about nothing other than connection and path-work, ways to connect, ways to reconnect if disconnection happens, and so on.

Especially the pip cards emphasize connection. In contrast, the trumps have a stronger individual force, where we actually see that the reason why the trumps are strong and appear individual is because 'connection' is already part of the program. Connection is not raised to higher status, when it already has high status.

Think about that. Think about the Emperor and how he relates to connecting. Do you think that the Emperor needs liking, before he goes on to give directives or delegate whatever there is to be done?

Historically, there have been Emperors obsessed with having people like them – think of Nero – but that has always proved to be the wrong approach.

All narcissists and others who merely claim super-connecting powers, yet demonstrate the opposite, end up beheaded or in the ditch. Why? Because they don't get connection; because they completely misunderstand what connection is essentially, namely, that it is all pervasive and encompassing.

You can never NOT connect. This is the subtle message of the pips cards. A pip card next to the Emperor who fulfils the function of leadership will talk about the ways in which leadership comes across in connective ways that underlie a specific structure.

In *The Power of the Trumps* I've written about the subtle power of the trump cards, but where the pips are concerned, what I find utterly fascinating is the fact that when the suits connect to the function of the trumps, or simply interconnect when no trumps are in the picture, what they do is teach a lesson in temporal and spatial awareness.

What I'm saying is this: All pip cards can be understood in terms of how we also understand temporal and spatial metaphors in a structural, binary, and numerical order: inside/outside, up/down, far/near, strong/soft, fast/slow, here/there, a little/a lot, sharp/dull, moveable/immovable, and so on—and yes, the latter, 'and so on' is also very much a representative of what pip cards can also act as: as conjunctions, appositions, pauses, ellipses, and adjectival and adverbial modifiers, including objections of this type: 'yes, but', and so on.

We tend to think that cards are invested with symbolic power. This is true to some extent, as there's no relation that we experience that's not already symbolic. Symbolism happens by default, through language. Language is representative of thoughts, not reality. It is also made up of random glyphs, not divine words.

Your very act of getting up in the morning, taking a shower, putting some perfume on and donning your best costume is a symbolic act of your readiness to go out and conquer the world.

You think that if you do this regularly, it will pay off and you end up belonging. But how is this thinking representative of reality, of what and who you are? It's not. All symbolic acts rest on dictations, not awarenss of original beingness.

Now, the difference between a symbol and a connector is that while a connector pervades what is the case, a symbol serves a master, as its whole premise rests on cultural convention.

A symbol doesn't arise out of vacuum. Someone creates it and then convinces others of its value. This is all fine until the point when this value is passed on as the thing itself, as reality. While some eat it raw, others resist.

In my work with the cards I see myself participating in this act of resisting. We use symbols to manipulate with emotions. Who stands to gain from this?

I try to address this question in a detached way, and then look at what other strategies for communication we have available to us that do not rely on a system of transacting with clichés.

The trumps tell us what is at stake. The pip cards make clear the connection between the agents involved and the way a narrative or story unfolds temporally and sequentially.

Let me give an example:

Symbolically for some, the Magician connects man to the divine. If your cards are the popular Waite-Smith Tarot you will nod to it, as this correspondence is part of the standard interpretation of the Magician. For others this connection is something that the Pope takes care of.

Symbolically, some connect the batons with fire, the coins with earth, the swords with thoughts, and the cups with water. I prefer my batons connected to air, as they tend to stick up in the wind, coins with fire, as you can't get one that's not forged in heat, swords with the earth as they can dig it too after the stabbing is done and the corpse needs burying.

The cups are pretty much a given, being obviously associated with all forms of liquids and libations, from blood to wine.

Functionally, however, we can see how we can bypass the symbolic constraint if we simply stick to noting what the suits do as a matter of course.

In terms of connection, I like to think of the four suits as representing bridges, the space between here and there. In photography this space is called 'negative space', the space where light meets darkness and shadows are created.

Think of how each of the four Aces initiates a suit, and represents a bridge over the negative space, the space without which there'd be no primordial act.

The Ace of Coins is the message: There is life and death. The more you cultivate both, the more polished you are.

The Ace of Cups is the shape of formlessness. Without flow resistance wins.

The Ace of Batons is the silent wind. It pushes you over into acceptance.

The Ace of Swords is the void of expectation. When the mind is free, the bones can create.

When we consider the pip cards as connectors, as bridges over troubled waters, we realize that what we once took as primary symbolic power is now turned over to the subtle realm, where the ambiguity of the symbol, to always mean more than it purports, is left to its own ambivalent device. No more drama.

With this sense of a symbol in mind consider these relations:

Yes / No (Red card / Black card)
A little / A lot (1, 10)
Big / Small (King, Page)
Up / Down (10, Ace)
Inside / Outside (Cups and Coins / Batons and Swords)
Slow / Fast (Cups and Coins / Batons and Swords)

What I'm doing here is point to metaphors we live by, that is to say, symbolic representations of verbal communication, space, time, distance, and speed.

Because we operate with nothing but the figurative and the symbolic, rules and conventions, there's no such thing as a cartomancy system that has answers for you through a set method that rules. Method rules nothing. You do. There's no such fixed thing as, 'if it's black, it's bad'. No, it's not. Not if you're a general in the army.

Question: Will I win the war? – This is a warrior asking.

Cards: Ace of Spades, 10 Spades.

Answer: Rejoice. You win the war.

Context and common sense determine the answer, not a book of random meanings on the internet. You can use lists of symbolic ideas instrumentally for inspiration, but you can never use them to create an original and coherent narrative that you own.

Let me make this explicit point: When you read cards in line for a coherent narrative or a specific aim that actually goes somewhere, something a lot of people find strenuous, what you do is actually activate this type of vocabulary, rather than the one that prioritizes lists of meanings devoid of the dynamic power of connecting.

Insofar as meaning is always relational, it makes little sense to upgrade it to a fixed status. There is no such thing as 'this means that'. There's only, 'this means that, at this point in time because there's a context that prompts it.' Context is King.

Here's a concrete example:

I'll read below a classical square of 13 cards from the French tradition, where the first card either emphasizes the significator, or is about the theme of the reading when no question is asked.

In my case here, and unlike my regular practice, I let the first card determine the theme.

The card at the bottom is the surprise. I always read this as a full stop or as a punchline to the narrative that I come up with.

I won't unpack the reading, as I normally do in the context of teaching a class, but rather just go for it, with complete disregard for standard symbolic meanings (obviously I'm well-aware of the fact that metaphors are also 'meanings' since they are part of linguistic conventions, but what I'm interested in here is more what **we** do with words rather than what words with do us).

Therefore, the only thing that interests me is sticking to the commonsensical knowledge of what I can logically infer is the function of each suit: **To drink with the cups, to transact with money, to build with batons, and to stab with the swords.**

In this book you will hear this mantra repeatedly. This is the only principle of the strategy of reading the cards, as it also relates to the idea of either scarcity (1, or a little) or plenitude (10, or a lot).

22

Let's see what the Magician, the first card down here, has to say. The premise for my reading takes point of departure in what I can presume a Magician does. As we're with a trump card here, we look at function: The Magician performs the function of demonstrating his skill at entertaining with the purpose of earning some money. This will be the theme of my reading.

Had the Ace of Swords been my first card, I would have said that the theme would be utter sharpness and cutting through whatever the other cards would show is the case.

Let's look at how we can proceed with having nothing in the head other than a sense of how we can manipulate with the temporal and spatial metaphors, as they lend themselves to the idea of connection (pips) in relation to function (trumps and court cards).

All in one line. You can be the judge of the extent to which this method of reading the pip cards makes sense, or is useful. I myself like it a lot, simply because it never wastes my time.

The Reluctant Magician

The Magician would rather not play with any sharp object (AS) in order to gain money (7D), but he can't run from the Queen of Swords who makes sure to remind him of how his painful indifference towards lovely offerings (4S, 10S, KC) leaves everything to Fortune that favours even the bold ones (Charioteer), who can never get enough of travelling to big cities (AC), in spite of the pain (5S) induced by having to dismount and exercise with a stick in order to make the jetlag go away, or to simply convince.

Ah, work! So much work for so little money. Thirteen cards and only one related to money...

Why so much pressure? Who likes to work so much?

Not the Magician. It's clear that this one here is not very efficient.

He starts out with a small stick between his fingers that's easy to manipulate, and ends up with a big one that he'll have trouble handling for the purpose of make-believe.

Granted, Houdini could make an entire city disappear, but insofar as our surprise card here is one of a heavy load, not one that suggests elegant poofs, we cannot infer that our Magician, who is not really into money, is of the same calibre as the most famous sleight-of-hand mentalists of the world.

In this short narrative, we have thus seen how flow can be created by just looking at the interplay between the function of the trump cards, the pips and the courts.

As there's symmetry in play at the formal level of this layout of cards, with the Magician beginning the story and the Page of Batons finishing it, we can also consider the latter as a 'lesser' version of the Magician.

Why? Because of rhyme, not because of aspect.

I've already suggested it. It's the one between the small stick in the Magician's hand and the big stick in the Page's hand.

Without this rhyme, we'd have to think of the Page as someone other than the Magician, someone who participates in the events that the Magician sets in motion.

As you will later see in the chapter on the court cards, I prefer it that the courts in a reading are given the status of 'other people', rather than see them as variations or aspects of the main significator.

But the reason why I want to introduce the idea of rhyme – an idea that comes from studies in poetry and poetics, psychoanalysis and dream interpretation, is because rhyme is very much also a connecting trope.

For instance, a more thorough break-down of the rhyming elements in our cards here, would further disclose how the Magician is connected or not, to his own sense of competence and where it's going, in terms of developing it.

There's a rhyming scheme here between three upstanding swords and three wheels. One sword for each wheel. That's worse than having a stick in your wheel.

So what can we infer? That this Magician is rolling with it in a smooth way? Hardly. Perhaps now we can see why he's so eager for sticks? But will sticks be of use, if rolling is what he wants? Not really.

What can we then further infer? That the Magician would be better off turning around and listening to the Queen in the picture. If she critiques his mental dribbling, poking at his golden nuggets, perhaps there's a reason.

What would happen if he didn't feel so threatened? Perhaps he wouldn't end up facing a wall of batons...

My theory is that the pip cards create flow in a reading by making us pay attention to how events and their progression are connected and by what means.

In this sense the pip cards can act as something other than their visual or symbolic character. They can say things like this:

However magically you try, if you don't know the value of sharpness as it relates to timing, you'll find that your effort is nothing but an exercise in displaying power by proxy.

This is another way of putting into words what I see is happening in the thirteen cards above.

Think of what creates coherence in your narratives, words such as 'however', 'and', 'but', 'consequently,' 'furthermore', 'full stop.' Now think of your pip cards representing such words. Try it.

I bet your readings will fly, as I also bet that you won't be able anymore to locate your fear of the pip cards, even if you tried.

With this in mind, let's move on to hearing what the court cards have to say, before we're ready to plunge into the more seductive and dancing power of the pips.

A Short Theory of the Court Cards

One of the questions that I often get in teaching cartomancy pertains to how we distinguish between the court cards. Who is who on the table, when the court cards show up?

I read the cards according to the function that I see each card embodies, whether I look at trumps, pip cards, or the court cards.

The suits are stylized ideas of our natural laws, as these interact with our way of coping with them.

— The wind is too strong? Well, build a house.

— With what?

— How about some trees?

Batons

Can we think of trees, in their stylized form as batons on the cards, as having an association to the idea of building, chopping wood and all that Zen-like attitude towards routine work that would be a good idea for us all to have, lest we should succumb to too much pressure? Indeed, we can think of the primary meaning of batons as 'work'.

What else do we know of trees?

They tend to grow tall in the air. The wind has a funny sound through the trees and their crowns.

— Would it make sense to associate the trees with air, then?

— I should think so.

What else? Trees have an interesting structure in their bark. Sometimes we can think of it as heavy skin. Rough. Unpolished.

The bark smells. It smells of the woods and the natural world. Sometimes animals take a piss on the trees, and then some funny looking weeds, both poisonous and not, grow by the roots. Hmm, I wonder what it all means. Very Saturnian.

If we gather the dead branches out in the woods, we can make a mighty fire with them. That is, after we build that luxury log house we dream about, the one that protects us from the strong western winds, or from the hustle and bustle of the city, its merchants and their transactions enabled by weirdly looking processed golden coins that tend to have the face of some schmuck leader or other imprinted on them.

Well, not real gold nowadays, as folks down history have long since given up on the necessity to have real gold passing through their hands whenever they need to trade shit for shine.

This wise decision was, of course, mediated by the merchants of the world, the sanguine folks, very good at rhetoric, and very good at convincing the wood people of the benefits of working for the government.

After all, when you're done with your own log house, maybe you can build ten or a hundred more just like the it.

All it requires is hard work. But you won't mind it, really, as what you're good at is in fact exactly that, chopping wood—whether for your own private use or for the public condo.

Who cares? You get paid, and work exhilarates you.

> — Is the King of Batons a King of work, then?
>
> — Why, yes he is.

What else can we know of the King of Batons, other than the fact that he smells, he works like a maniac and demands the same?

He plans a lot—all that wood needs counting—he builds connections, and he's good at figuring out which stick fits what hole. That's quite enough already.

Essentially, however, all we need to do is think this: The suit of Batons equals a whole lot of wood.

Coins

Whoever is in charge of the coins, and now virtual banking transactions, belongs to the group of very smart folks. Their brains are irrigated by blood in an almost mystical way.

Well, so it goes with all the trickster gods. If they're good at anything, that'd be commerce and how to make others work for them. Yep. You gotta have a lot of brain power to convince the wood folks to work for you. And then for what exactly?

For losing the very thing that feeds their need for work. How many more forests must go down? Too many.

The result? A cold and dry temperament.

The wood folks will get depressed — 'melancholic' they used to call it — and will soon be in need of making a new transaction: More work in exchange for a soul.

If the coin, Mercurial type of folks will not be able to provide the service, they will be sure to direct the wood folks to a professional.

They are after all masters of fixing ambivalence. They know everything about crossroads, whether asphalt or clay.

The coin folks are **wired**.

Cups

The water people are the phlegmatics of the world.

— What's that?

— Well, that is desire with a capital D.

Here comes Venus, the Goddess of Love and Money. We all want that, but some want that really badly. They will pray to the moon and back for it.

Just think of what we do with water in its stylized form as we find it on the cards in the form of cups filled with liquid, or as hearts.

With cups we make a toast, invite friends for a nice ritual of liba-tion, and then watch how everybody will get their tongues untied, giving way to a whole lot of repressed emotions and desires, disclosing also just what a mighty power the power of insatiable desire is.

If the wood folks come to the water folks, the water folks will know how to show sympathy. On rare occasions they will show compassion, Jupiter style, but sympathy is more frequent.

After all, since the water folks crave stuff all the time, and they are **the** masters at craving, there's only so much empathy they can display.

But they will be able to hear the pulse in your veins, pumping through your heart.

This pulse is close to what the water folks are good at identifying: Circulation. Any flow of blood is their specialty.

Swords

Spilling blood. That's the domain of the choleric folks, the Mars folks, the warriors, the ones who are good with a sword in their hands.

They have one mantra only, which they repeat incessantly: 'Off with their heads.'

When they're done with all that chopping of heads, guess what, some digging is necessary.

Where do you suppose that all those spades represented on playing cards come from? The digging of the earth.

Swords and earth. Do you see the connection? The two malefics, Mars and Saturn. You don't want to go against them. Their presence in any layout spells out **trouble**.

Imagine to live in this paradox:

In order to know the coldness of the earth, you need to have a very hot head, blinding your actions. 'En garde!,' the Solar fixated French cloak and dagger folks used to shout all the time in those noble days of chivalric retribution, using the hottest passion and the coldest head, thus inverting the order of things: Hot head and cold passion.

But who cares, as long as somebody dies. Exhilarating.

If the choleric swordsmen play their cards right, they might even get either the wood folks to dig the graves for the dead, or the water folks to officiate the burial, or more likely to shed some tears on behalf of the community.

Where do you think that all those traditions of lamentation come from? Keening, anyone? The Irish are very good at it. Not to mention the Romanians.

Who Died?

I don't know about you, but I have participated in many funerals, including those of my parents where I've witnessed the following:

The wood folks provided the coffins and the external planning of what to do with the dead corpse, how to dress it and all that. Work.

The water folks provided the libation and the tears. Family comforting.

The coin folks took our money and promised to facilitate help in case of a nervous breakdown. Fast messengers.

The earth folks dug the graves with their spades, and nailed the coffins.

Friend or Foe?

We all sit at the table together, eating or stabbing each other if the drinks go to our heads.

We sit together in church, or by somebody's grave. We comfort each other, or slander each other. We love each other, or kill each other.

The suits represent the four universal types we all recognize from our walks of life. Some are lumpers, some are splitters.

The court cards leading the numbers are all faithful representatives of their kingdoms.

King of Coins, King of Cups, King of Batons, King of Swords

What does a **King** do? Sit on it, sit on his achievements.

A King is above having to prove himself, to consolidate stuff, to make transactions. He delegates. He has others do these things for him.

Therefore he embodies a symbol of power in its static manifestation. If Cups, man of love; if Batons, man of work; if Coins, man of money; if Swords, man of war.

The **Knight** is an emblem of consolidating the King's business in an active way. He's into developing.

The difference between a symbol of power and an emblem of development is one of rank. The Knight acts on behalf of, whereas the King is at the top, commanding and controlling power.

The **Queens**, as the creators of the world, fulfill their function of being guardians of sacred knowledge, and hence of truth.

They embody a different kind of power that's aligned with how we see with the logical eyes and how we see with the so-called illogical eyes—this latter idea, especially as seen from the perspective of culture.

Pages are agents at the mercy of others. They are sons and daughters, messengers, or apprentices.

Their presence in a string of cards, especially if the string consists of the highest rank court cards, can indicate the thoughts or emotions of these higher powers.

The Page of Cups can be an emotional extension of what the Queen of Cups is thinking about, or what she intends to act towards.

They can also be seen as stages towards the manifestation of the mighty power that a King possesses.

If the King of Swords doubts as to whether he must engage and go to war or not, the presence of the Page of Swords in the sequence of cards will most likely confirm this ambivalence, the Page of Swords being a nasty little thing, always intent on splitting relations, rather than finishing them off the honorable way, in a duel, or by actually going to war.

The Page of Coins aspires to make money, but he lacks the cunningness of the King of Coins.

At the other pole, the Page of Cups is always sweet and floundering, encouraging his single mother to find a husband for herself.

Oh, the sympathy that can turn nasty, if the Queen is too impressionable herself, and unable to discern what the truth is.

Truth or Dare?

I see the idea that the Queen equals truth as related to the way we make a distinction between the public and the private spheres.

At least that's my conclusion after reflecting on the cunning folk cartomancy, often referenced by others in various books and online resources, but without full explanations as to why we equate a court card with a certain idea (see, for instance, a favorite of mine, Dawn Jackson's Hedgewytch method, which, although logically wonderful and sound, often falls short of examining the root of the logical thread behind why we say what we say).

Queen of Coins, Queen of Cups, Queen of Batons, Queen of Swords

This is fair enough, as the best way to go about it is to think for yourself. Let us assume, then, that since a queen is not considered 'a man of action' she may sit on the domain of thought, thus approving of our attitude of thinking for yourself.

Consequently, after I was done with my own share of thinking about it, here is what I have arrived at:

Traditionally men have occupied the public sphere — well, they still do — and women the private sphere.

Where is it more likely to find the truth? Obviously not in the public sphere where politicians set the agenda. The truth is the closest to us, our private place, our soul. Who has access to this? Women. That's my reasoning.

I haven't seen others talk about it in this specific way, though it is likely that you can stumble over similar, albeit much more abstract notions.

In books about esoteric tarot people refer to the court cards as having to do with an expression of the within and without dichotomy, or indeed as following the hermetic axiom: 'As above, so below' (see Marcus Katz's work).

In other tarot books that have a psychological bent, you'll come across the court cards as described in terms of their helping or non-supportive attitude (from counselors to abusers, critics, victims, champions, and so on; see Kate Warwick Smith's work).

Functions

As far as I'm concerned, the court cards qualify to **perform a function** all according to the suit they embody and the context of the question.

Whether the King of Swords is a bad magician today and a good magistrate tomorrow will be something we can determine according to how we see the essential qualities of the suit of swords in alignment with the context of the question.

Furthermore, the distance between action and truth, the public sphere and the private sphere, and men and women is also determined by the surrounding cards.

If your question is about your need to know some truth, or it has an investigative character, then the presence of the Queen will tell you what you need to focus on.

If the Swords, the truth is distorted; if the Cups the truth flows. The other suits give you a 'maybe'.

It's the question and the context that give you the answer to when the Queen acts as an emblem of truth or not.

What is the question, exactly?

If the question is one about how to handle the truth, then the presence of the Queen of Swords alongside the King of Cups suggests difficulty in admitting to suffering from blind spots.

The Page of Swords alongside the Queen of Swords suggests intentional lying, where the Page modifies the Queen's thoughts or intent for the worse.

The Knight of Batons can be a real estate agent when in the presence of the King of Coins, and so on.

Beyond cultural pre-conditioning, when we have to determine who all these court people are, populating our spreads, we can remind ourselves that we can also see with something other and more than our cognitive capacity to decode, interpret, and make aesthetic evaluations, or judgments.

We can see how, following the suits, we are more prone to becoming obsessed with money than with work, and committing a crime of passion than passionately going to war.

The reason for this is related to the closeness of the four stylized ideas in the cards of love, money, work, and war to our own concerns.

Coins make us sweaty and hot. The heart can beat fast and rush us into action. Work schemes won't excite us nearly as much as money schemes, and war hardly ever wins in the affairs of the heart—though heads may fall.

Swords and batons are long, and we hold them at arm's length. We hold coins in our palms, and the blood in our veins keeps us alive.

What is our most immediate need? Shelter and love. Money buys us the house and the bedroom. We only need to go to war, or compete, if the neighbor has her eyes on our property.

The Self and the Other

Court cards always represent other people. They hardly ever represent 'aspects' of ourselves, not even when we try to stretch our esoteric politeness.

Court cards as aspects of us are pretty useless, and in mundane questions they never work. Telling someone who gets the Queen of Cups and the Queen of Coins side by side that this indicates how she can sometimes be full of love and other times full of brains will hit a nerve, for sure.

But how specific is that? Aren't we all like that? Aren't we sometimes loving and sometimes innovative?

Generalities never move anyone.

Think in specific terms beyond the cliché.

Pick a significator

The best is to go old school, and always pick a significator before laying out any larger spread of cards.

The significator must be aligned first with the profession of the person asking the question, and then, following tradition, with the physical traits.

Traditionally, a blondish, a red head, or a woman with white hair, is represented by the Queen of Coins. If she's a professor, or manages the bank, you're set. I start with this latter attribution.

The Queen of Cups is a mother, or a woman working in healthcare. She also tends to be blond—go figure…

The Queen of Batons knows her business, and handles practical matters with mastery. She is an enterprising brunette.

The Queen of Spades is the darkest in complexion, and works as a judge or a bad witch—the question decides whichever.

The King of Batons is a manager or boss, of dark complexion, and the King of Cups a father, a counsellor, or a priest, a blond man.

The King of Swords is a magistrate, a policeman, George Clooney in *Ocean's Eleven*, or a mentalist. Usually he is the darkest in complexion.

The King of Coins is a financial tycoon, freckled or reddish blond towards olive complexion.

The Knight follows suit regarding profession and physical traits, and acts as a delegate.

If the King is a general, the Knight is his soldier (Swords).

If the King is a bank director, the Knight speculates on Wall Street (Coins).

If the King is a cardiologist, the Knight is a seducer (Cups).

If the King is a developer, the Knight is a forest ranger (Batons).

Pages study or deliver messages (Coins), meddle in others' affairs without concern (Swords), work for a herbalist (Batons), or day-dream (Cups).

There's hardly any ambiguity as to who does what and for what purpose.

Because of this purpose, the court cards give us a sense of direction. In their presence we're not in any situation that makes us doubt: 'Maybe this is also an aspect of you immolating yourself.'

ROY·DE·DENIER·

ROYNE·DE·DENIER·

CHEVALIER·DE·DENIERS·

VALET·DE·DENIER·

The Court Cards in Readings

Let's look briefly at a couple of examples:

The first is the classical square of 9 cards.

This example comes from a reading for a woman writer whose field is Western esotericism and occultism. I picked the Queen of Diamonds as her significator. I did not put her aside, but left her in the pack.

Generally, if the significator shows up in the spread, it will indicate that the querent will take an active part in the dynamics of what is being asked about.

If not, then we can see it as a sign that the querent will be impacted on by factors that are more external to her concern.

Here is the woman's question:

What exactly characterizes the people I write for, and how can I best serve them?

How do I develop a stronger sense of belonging?

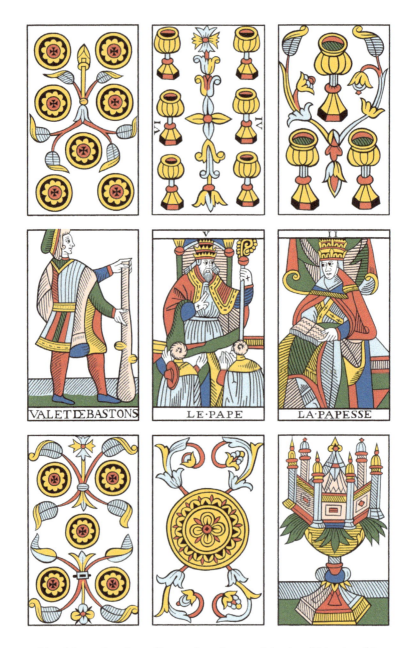

7 Coins, 6 Cups, 3 Cups, Page of Batons, Pope, Popess, 5 Coins, Ace of Coins, Ace of Cups

In this 9-card tableau we got only one court card.

This is not so surprising, given the nature of the question to identify the traits of the folks the querent wishes to belong to and serve. The court cards tend to pop more frequently in questions about family or relationships at work.

I picked this example, however, even though it only features one court card here, the Page of Batons, simply because I found that it participated in giving a very literal answer.

As the significator, the Queen of Coins, didn't show up in the spread, we can infer that this is due to her having some doubts, indeed, as to where her writing belongs. But it's clear that her skills belong with the spiritual folks.

The center card is the Pope, flanked to the left by the Page of Batons, handling a rough staff, and the Popess, or the High Priestess, handling a book.

The Page here is simply the altar boy, who is also out in the yard fixing things. The cards in the middle spell it out quite clearly that the querent's folk is church folk, or ritualists.

What we can note here is that we have quite a preponderance of coins and cups over batons and swords. Swords are not even represented at all.

We're thus with the suits close to us, giving us access to what we hold in our hands in a more intimate way, cups and coins, rather than the distant swords and batons.

If we were to describe the people our querent is interested in writing for, we'd say the following:

They have money problems, but know the way of the heart and how to have a good time (7 Coins, 6 Cups, 3 Cups).

As we're with the coins here, representing mental power within the context of the church and ritual, we can impose a spiritual reading on the card of the 7 Coins as it relates to divination and fortunetelling, clairvoyance and mystical vision.

Basically, if you're mental in the church that means that you're a mystic of sorts.

In a magical setting, the number 7 cards are the only cards that can change status, from indicating trouble, in a mundane situation, to suggesting shapeshifting; vision if coins, practical and talismanic magic if batons, mysticism and gnosis if cups, and 'black' magic if swords.

At the core of this tribe is a spiritual leader, attended by his apprentice and a wise woman (Page of Batons, Pope, Popess).

The community may struggle with money, but when the folks here get their hands on it, they spend it all on themselves, and then take a ride on the flying carpet towards the One love (5 Coins, Ace of Coins, Ace of Cups).

These folks are good at casting circles, creating some good sigils, and making lavish offerings in the form of libations, judging by the looks at the Ace of Coins and the Ace of Cups.

If ever a spiritual community is led by the motto: 'Love is all you need', we get a confirmation of it here.

The Page's work consists of swinging his bat between visions and relics. With lots of vigor.

Money goes into setting up altars that look good and smell good, or other type of ritual jewelry that spiritual folks like to adorn themselves with (7 Coins, Page of Batons, 5 Coins).

The Pope leads the way and delivers messages of roundness: 'God bless everyone, and don't fall off the magic carpet. Have another ritual drink' (6 Cups, Pope, Ace of Coins; 6s are for travel).

Everyone enjoys the party under the watchful eye of the High Priestess, who makes sure that the Holy Grail is filled to the brim with the good stuff (3 Cups, Popess, Ace of Cups).

This tribe is into love and visions, money magic, and wisdom.

Who wouldn't want to belong here? A good message for our Queen of Diamonds, the querent, who is already on this path, having written some short stories that had magic as a topic.

But she wanted to know how she could make herself more visible to this tribe—upon observing that her presence was missing from this party.

Basically she was concerned that she wrote for people who didn't really see her, while nonetheless consuming her offerings.

I turned up the bottom card from the cut deck. It disclosed the 7 Cups.

'More love,' I said. Make an offering, and stand out. You belong already. The 7 Cups is a card of spirituality, so start contributing to filling that big chalice in the middle with your own libations. It will be appreciated.'

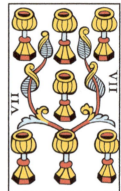

But then I added the note that, traditionally, whenever the Popess shows up in the layout, she has a relation to the querent, if not representing the querent directly, then in an implicit way.

Here the link between the Popess and her book and the Queen of Coins and her book was more direct, given the writing profession.

Quite literally, as the Popess is dealing with books, she mirrors what the Queen of Coins does: Reads and writes books, and thinks a lot.

As you can see, then, although we didn't have any reason to wonder about agency here, and fret about the question of who is who, we could read the one court card here precisely according to the function that it performs:

A young man participating in making the spiritual community magical, and also giving a direct message to the querent about the more nuanced aspects of the community of people she is serving, ritual being one of their primary concerns.

My advice was to write more intricately about all aspects of 'church' life, and suggest what talismanic value love has for organized spirituality.

My Family

The second example features a line of 5 cards, for which I picked no significator in advance.

A man wanted to know:

What is our common goal in our family?

8 Coins, Queen of Coins, Page of Cups, Magician, Force

Following the direction of the gazes in this spread we notice the following: The goal is money.

It starts with a financial-like meeting presided over by the woman of money, the Queen of Coins, who brings her own contribution to it.

A loving young man, the Page of Cups, follows this woman (not his blood mother, as the querent also validates), and brings his emotions to the table.

The Magician watches the parade, and follows the Page of Cups. He is probably also thinking: Can I make more money?

The Queen is closer to the money than the Magician, so money is more important to her than it is to him. He is gazing towards money from some distance, but it looks like he enjoys more the idea that he can just make money happen out of the blue. That's what a Magician does, after all.

The last card in this line indicates a tension. Although the common goal seems to be chasing after money, the Magician is not on the same page as the Queen and the Page. He even seems to be wondering: What's this fascination with money that the Queen mirrors, and the Page desires?

The card of Force shows a female trying to tame an animal. A force seems to pull the Magician away from the monetary goal, enticing him to recalibrate his focus on something wilder and more essential than the culture of money.

As he is not aware of this force—he's not looking towards what else is there—it is no wonder that he ends up seeking the service of a fortuneteller, who can help him sort out the family circus.

A good thing we're here to serve.

A Community of Agents

To sum up, the court cards are agents helping us or blocking us from achieving what we want. They can counsel us, sell us down the river, talk about us behind our backs, or stab us. They are mortals who act in their own right, just like we do.

A good reading of the court cards will take into consideration the dynamics of the interrelation between ourselves and others, our contexts and platform for action and those of the others.

Sometimes we mirror ourselves in what the court cards do, but these other agents are never us.

We come into the world, we live, and we die. While quite alone on our life path, we encounter others who tell us their stories.

This is the function of the court cards: To tell us a story that teaches us something about ourselves, how to live and die better, how to better breathe the air we share, and how to think of our own role and place on this planet.

If we're still confused, we can call in the trumps, or let the numbers speak what there is to speak, in that beautiful and abstract manner that only numbers are capable of.

In the next chapter, however, we're going to look at the ways in which numbers can be brought closer to our mundane experiences, while retaining their infinite, mathematical potential.

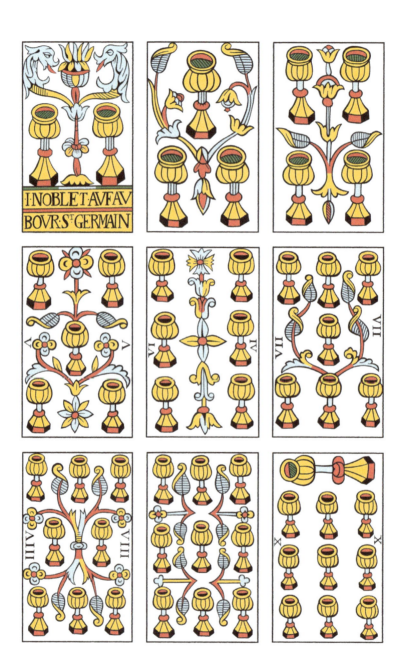

The Wishing Well

Everybody is familiar with the Buddhist greeting: 'May all sentient beings be happy.'

The Christians also say, 'I'll pray for you', if they hear you're in trouble.

'May you live 10000 years,' the Japanese shout, martial arts style, when they want to cheer with a hurrah.

Some African and Arabic cultures greet women with these words: 'May you have many children.'

Now, if you thought of taking any of these wishes literally, I bet you'd be horrified.

The truth is that we can never generalize.

What is happiness for some is disaster for others. Some get high adrenaline from being in trouble, while making it even to 80 without any trouble is already a tall order.

Not to mention the number of emancipated women I know from African and Arabic cultures for whom the idea of having any children at all is already is enough to cause suicidal anxiety.

What does it mean to pray for others, and how beneficial is it?

We leave this question of ethics aside, as it's not the most interesting. What is interesting is this:

How can we mean what we say, even if the saying is part of innocent – we think – cultural encounters and exchange?

'It's about emptying the house,' you hear old people say, while you also notice the mechanism of clinging to every possession like there was no tomorrow. Not to mention the fact that if you care to observe the actual behaviour further, you will also notice that while the claim is made, five years down the road the place houses twice as many things as before.

§

People come to me with this concern:

'I want to stop procrastinating. How can I stop procrastinating?'

Before I lay down any cards, I ask them: 'How much do you actually mean it? Do you even know what it takes to actually mean it?'

'Err, what do you mean? I just want to stop procrastinating,' people say, looking at me in a baffled way.

I offer this thought:

There's a difference between wishing for it, being motivated for it, and having an intention for it.

The trouble with wishing something is that while it often discloses an intention, the wish is devoid of motivation.

What motivates us to pray for people, to help them, to pray for ourselves, or to help ourselves?

If we're not clear in the head as to what motivates us, there's one sure consequence: Our intention to act on this motivation will be equally muddled. This leaves wishing altogether to the intangible realm.

When consulting the cards, the thing to remember is that some questions necessitate prerequisites, or awareness of a particular positioning.

If you want to know how you can stop procrastinating, before you even ask that question, you must know something about what motivates you:

What is implicit in your desire?
Is the implicit motivation clear, so your intention will be clear?
How connected is your motivation to your intention?

A procrastinator thus wanted to know: 'How can I mean what I say,?' as a prerequisite to reading the cards for the actual steps and strategy towards putting a stop to his idle situation.

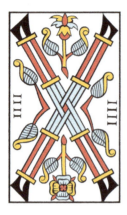  

Three cards fell on the table:

4 Batons, 8 Swords, 7 Batons

After constancy and painful expectation, there's release of action. It's normal to expect to mean what you say... But...

You can only mean what you say, if you firmly check with your points of pressure, and then act upright and resolutely.

How far does your elastic stretch? Before you stretch it, are your corners covered, and your feet well anchored in your motivation?

You'd think it takes effort to maintain a solid stance. After all, saying that you mean something doesn't equal action, or immediate following through.

But if action follows your words promptly, then you're set.

You can mean what you say if you let the nerve of your intention stand in clear relation to your motivation.

You can mean what you say when you let your word be unnerving and your action be unwavering.

Don't think that you can beat yourself up about it, or stab yourself slowly and quietly in a cast iron cauldron.

You can mean what you say in the exact moment you also show up for it. One way or another.

There's no tomorrow. There's no promise: 'I'll do it.'

There's only stepping up to this reality:

If you don't mean it, don't say it.

Humor Me

There's hardly any astrology website out there that doesn't emphasise the moods of the Moon.

Let's see. I'm writing this while the Moon is in Libra, the sign of harmony, love, and money.

The advice is to make sure not to alienate anyone by falling into some ambivalent trap, or what's worse, by making any contradictory claims.

By the same token, if the Moon is in Leo, then the advice is to flatter people, give compliments, and engage in boosting everyone's ego. You do this, and they will like you.

Very useful advice. But...

Someone please humor me: How does this type of advice, however useful, tie in with what I was just suggesting in the previous chapter about meaning what we say?

If we pay compliments to people at a certain point in time because this time is ruled by planetary movements, then what does this say about our integrity at large, especially if we deem that now is a good idea to pay someone a compliment? What if the condition for such a gesture is right now, not a month from now?

I'm not asking this question when the moon is in Libra today because I'm bent on being contrary to the useful advice – thus also running the risk of upsetting people – or because I want to express my sense of righteousness.

I'm asking simply because I don't see how, if someone deserves a compliment for their looks when the Moon is in Virgo, then I can't do it because, according to the mood of the Moon, that would be the time to offer a critique instead, not a compliment.

What does it mean to adopt moods and humors that are not our own? Sometimes I have this discussion with my own astrology teacher, a very serious gentleman who only sends me emails when Mercury is not afflicted by some nasty aspect to the Moon or some other planet.

This makes me think of the idea of constancy against the background of influencing others or manipulating them.

Humors are the opposite of what we might think of as a constant and solid spine; one that doesn't bend in the direction of giving people what they want to hear all the time.

I'm not advocating for an inflexible spine, as I can take my cue from nature: A bamboo tree bending in the wind will be infinitely stronger than the oak that doesn't.

So constancy doesn't mean being inflexible. It simply means having a position that's aligned with your own humor completely independently of which direction the wind blows.

But if you don't know what position you adopt, or even what humor you're in also according to what's available to you, then what?

No matter how much self-disciplining you impose on yourself where your strategies of self-empowerment are concerned, the truth is that you're always subject to internal and external conditions that may run completely counter to what you want to achieve.

How do you figure it out? Some look at what others do. Imitating especially the best is always a good strategy, and even better if you can perfect their craft. But it becomes a lot less good when you start comparing yourself to others in relation to what you project is personal business for you. In the moment you take things personally, you become judgmental. Who will want to follow you when you're humoured like that?

§

A constant feature on the internet these days is related to growing an audience. Entire courses and workshops are offered on how you can humor others, which is also where observing planetary alignments along with your algorithmic stats comes in.

In my reading practice, it's not uncommon that I get this question for the cards:

'How can I grow my Instagram, Twitter, or Facebook audience? How can I make more people visit my webpage so they can see my offerings?'

I won't go into the countless types of advice to this effect, as the internet is already flooded with all sorts, but I will point to what you may want to consider as a matter of course.

A better question to ask is the question that opens you up to realizing that whatever impression arises to the mind, it is part and parcel of what you yourself project and perceive is the case.

Where does this leave the humor of others, or that of the Moon in terms of our indulging it? It leaves it to the world of alternative facts.

In a way, a community invested in cartomancy, astrology, and other divinatory arts is already a community of alternative facts. What makes it magical is precisely the alternative. The alternative doesn't prioritize solutions based on this reasoning: 'If people like you, they'll follow you, and then they'll buy everything from you.' That's not how it works.

The alternative prioritizes the game of potentiality, the fact that while we may consider the moods of the Moon for the sake of the game, what we're up against is our own God-given sense of emptiness, of the blank surface that we can magically paint on in any way our linguistic competence helps us. Without the words to say it, there's no magic. Without words to think it, there's no imagination.

With this in mind, how about we ask the cards this question?

How can I be constant against the shifting moods and positions of others? How can I remain immune in the face of 'now they like me, now they don't?'

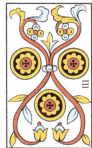

Page of Coins, 3 Coins, King of Cups, Queen of Coins

Some assets you show, some you don't.

You can remain constant when you bank on symmetrical relationships. If you give one, the other must give one.

What is buried in the ground, can stay in the ground.

You can think of your third coin as insurance against the time when the one who used to like you, now turns his back at you in order to seek the favour of the one who is older and more interesting financially.

You can't control what people like or dislike.

The best is to know that you yourself can be above likes and dis-likes. Make your transactions in accordance.

If 'liking' happens, it happens, and if it doesn't, it doesn't.

It may well be that your audience won't grow if there's dislike of what you have to offer, but if you're above liking and disliking, how is that going to affect you?

Connect with your inner glow. Let the underground valuable turn into a king's purse.

If money happens, it happens, and if it doesn't, it doesn't. You are not the money you make, or the money you have. That is your constant. That is your undivided mind.

Believable Stories

If we can establish that what we do is not subject to likes and dislikes, then we can think about what we know, how sharp our knowledge is, what stories we create based on what we know, and how believable these stories are.

I like the idea of sharpness here simply because, let's face it, armed with a sharp object you're very believable.

Imagine having a confrontation. You have a shiny blade in your hand. The other holds a coin. Imagine saying to the one with the coin in her hand: 'How do you like this?' Or, 'how much do you dislike this?' The other would think you're probably stupid to ask about likes and dislikes. She may even blurt at you: 'What's it to you whether I like this or not? You're a warrior, not an aesthete. Come and get me.'

This would be a normal reaction to your context. As a warrior you normally create a story of threat, strategy, and war. You can't be bought and you can't be seduced. Thus what the other one sees is the potential that you chop her up and then run with her coin too. This is a very believable story, also because it happens all the time. Repetition creates icons and stereotypes.

Some stories are created beyond the possibility to negotiate. They have value by virtue of being believable.

I'm fascinated by stories of Samurai. Especially the part when they walk about, and then live and die even without ever having to draw their sword. People watch them from afar, from what they consider is a safe distance. This watching has the character of a declarative statement: 'I believe you.'

The samurai and the figure of the ronin, or the unattached swordsman, have entered our collective memory and popular culture by telling what is essentially a very basic story anchored in projected and imaginary dialogues that have a simple exchange as their premise.

ROY·DESPEE   ROYNE DE DENIER

The Samurai: 'I can cut you'.

The other: 'I believe you.'

End of business. Each minds their own.

Now, when it becomes interesting is when the other covets what the Samurai knows. While a merchant, man or woman, is more prone to negotiation: 'My coin for your sword?,' a warrior is not: 'Are you kidding me? Not a chance.'

The solution is to propose discipleship. Sometimes the Samurai agrees: 'Ok, I'll teach you.' But when this happens you'll see that it always starts on a premise of establishing negative value, with the Samurai being NOT AT ALL interested in who or what you are, and what you think of him.

I get a kick out of having figured it out for myself that what the Samurai knows best is how to say NO. He says NO to a life of dictations by saying YES to death, the ultimate negation of life and all cultural conventions whether they be determined by rank, gender, age, or race.

As this is a territory I've been exploring for some time now in my work with cards and Zen, I won't go into the many fascinating details about it, but I want to offer here a snippet of insight into what I take from such cutting lessons, as it relates to how we create believable stories (if your interest is piqued, however, stay tuned for my planned book on martial arts cartomancy).

§

What I appreciate about the magical community is that it's filled with creative and innovative people. Many are successful entrepreneurs with whom I often have marketing conversations.

Most are into YES, into creating so-called positive value. I say NO. This is my magical weapon for many wars. Not that I go to war all the time, but I like the idea of following whatever I have come to realize about my nature. I don't follow dictations.

Since I've left the academy for the less prestigious job of working for myself too, I've been confronted with many fears. Not mine, to be sure, as I say NO to fear, but others.

'You must do this, or that, say yes to this, yes to that, say yes to your customers, say yes to what you want, say yes to what they want,' and so the story goes.

All fine up to the point when I'm strongly advised to address people directly, call them by their names, address their individual needs, imagine what they desire, and bow to the illusion that 'it's all about them'.

Well, you see, I don't fall for automated marketing emails that address me by my name, that assume to know what I want, what I struggle with, what my needs are, and what I imagine about embodying a particular desired identity, if any at all.

Just as I don't get impressed by such tactics, I can't imagine anyone I address in my own email campaigns does. So I don't. I don't assume.[1] In other words, I find myself following absolutely none of the strategies that marketing gurus out there devise in the name of surviving in business.

---

1 I've dedicated a chapter to this idea as well in *The Power of the Trumps*.

I pretty much say no to all of it. I say no to the idea of catering to imaginary clients and potential clients. A potential client is exactly that, potential, not reality.

My own so-called surviving strategy has been very simple: 'Those who are like me will find me.' I don't put any effort into imagining who, out there, might be my potential client, who might read this book, who might take my cartomantic classes.

I do what I do and fling it to the public to the best of my ability. If people want it, excellent, if they don't want it, excellent. There's no difference in my attitude towards what I expect. Because I expect exactly nothing.

What I put energy into is what I create and how well. No one can be a better judge than myself of what I create, how well, and where it all comes from. This premise alone means that I entertain no illusion about how many or who exactly I 'reach', simply because I'm always alone in what I do and what I think.

I don't fall for the illusion of 'community', as interestingly enough, when it comes down to it, it turns out that the community minds its own business at individual level and separate level in spite of contrary claims. Last I've checked, communities are not exactly Zen.

Valuing this aloneness means a great deal, as it affords you the space that's completely devoid of making assumptions and presumptions. Second-guessing is not an option either.

This also means that, in principle, nothing of what you create and put out there into the world is ever up to negotiation. You think it is, but in reality it isn't.

Imagine living with this realization, and consequently just doing your thing, and entertaining zero concerns about potential responses, whether positive or negative. You can call this a conscious act of embodying the attitude of 'take it or leave it'.

Why does this work? Simply because of the realization that if there's feedback or response to what you create, then this particular feedback or response will also very much be the manifestation of someone else's aloneness – even when this aloneness happens that it's the expression of some consensus opinion.

If a hundred people consume your offerings, you can have one hundred percent confidence that, at the end of the day, what you sit with is a hundred opinions, impressions, critiques, or praises. So much for being purposeful in your business and reaching the one and only...

The way in which we perceive the world is not through an assessment of the world such as it is, but rather through a realization that what we perceive at any given time is our own perception of perception.

In its undiluted form Zen teaches that we don't perceive the world. We perceive our perception of the world. So we're always one level lower than 'the thing itself'.

Given this realization, it makes very little sense for you to create anything in the name of what you perceive that even your own desire is.

As far as I'm concerned, I try to not have any desire. I just do what I perceive I'm good at, which is to give sharp advice, say no, transact for no illusion, and expect no miracle.

The only miracle that excites me is the nothingness of it all; the fact that nothing has any substance.

Given this premise, I like to move mountains, speak to their silent wisdom, and pulverize the hell out of expectation.

I practice entering the void because that is my vehicle to the absolute beyond. In this state of mind, there's no mind, there's no compromise, there's no 'be careful not to offend,' there's no illusion. Things are as they are. Take it or leave it.

What are your questions?

Cards are like calligraphy. They can disclose the nature of the self when the self is beyond the fear of rising to expectations. This is bad for the mind that will always find strategies of trumping the nature of the self by creating anxiety.

Pip cards and court cards are like the dots that connect the major narrative lines puncturing them with the unexpected.

In the context of working for yourself, what questions do you ask your cards in your strategy of going about it, of creating believable stories?

Are your questions client related?

Who are my people?

What do they want?

Are your questions product related?

What am I selling?

What is the value of what I'm selling?

Are your questions problem related?

What problems do I imagine I'm solving?

Is my effort informed by any 'savior' syndrome that I also imagine is aligned with what I promise?

Are your questions distribution related?

How is my image and that of my product in the world, on social media, or some other such channels?

What narrative does my product tell?

What story do I invest in?

Lastly, are your questions 'self' related, or 'other' related?

What illusions do I maintain?

How prone am I to falling for slogans such as: 'It's all about them', 'the customer is always right', 'know everything about your customer', 'be ruthless'?

What is my vehicle to the realization of truth, which is another way of asking, what is my vehicle towards seeing things as they are?

Sometimes I run a check with myself and read a set of three cards for each of these questions, or some other similar ones. Though I have to admit that since my philosophy is simple and rather one-sided as I don't negotiate much, what I check is just strength:

I check the strength of my attitude of 'take it or leave it,' as I don't want it to be the manifestation of indifference or even resentment.

I check the strength of my acceptance of what is, whether this is feedback that translates into monetary value and appreciation or critique.

I check the strength of my fearlessness and what informs my discernment. If I'm cautious, what is it a manifestation of? Fear, or wisdom?

Nine cards for your strategy

Doing a 9-card reading for these considerations can be rewarding, as you get to see the dynamics of morphing: Your attitude and perception morphing with the state of things such as they are, not such as they are part of whatever narrative you serve yourself.

Here's an example of a question that combines interrelated statements: One about your skills, another about your attitude towards what you do with your skills, and a third about your concern with how what you do is received by the public. Disregard this latter concern, however, if your business has a Zen-oriented premise, insofar as any meditation practice that has self-analysis in focus maintains no illusion of separation between 'you' and 'them'.

> What is the best business strategy for me beyond mainstream marketing dictations?

> What is my vehicle towards embodying a completely fearless attitude towards what I'm creating, for what purpose and for whom?

Before we proceed with the reading of cards here, it may be helpful to keep in mind that although we talk about having a 'purpose' and 'direction', what we're actually talking about when we use such concepts is just a mirror of what we project as a manifestation of our aims.

In reality, 'purpose' and 'direction' are words that belong to the register that gives us more cause for anxiety than comfort. They are not invested in our ideal attitude towards maintaining neutrality vis-à-vis our identifications with the image of the self that we create, an image that is always arbitrary and dependent on shifting contexts for self-realization.

Let us have a look, as the cards below prove to be quite fun.

The Queen of Spades has turned her back from having an emotional conversation with the Magician. 'I've had it', the 10 Cups suggest – here's your first connector acting as a full stop. While the two can be said to have been in agreement at some point, they entertain no illusions now – though the Magician still makes a living selling it by virtue of his very function.

There's money to be made, and there's drive towards it. While the Knight of Swords charges ahead, ready to dig for the coin that's not in conversation with the two above it, Justice has no opinion about it.

The Knight can trust her to back him, however, as we can infer that with Justice in his line he can now make the right decision. This may be useful, as you never know with the swords people and how much they ultimately dig financial interests; they are more prone to sabotaging them.

Here I like the suggestion that if you know the value of what you're offering, and you're fair about it, then the only natural thing that you can expect to happen is to get more of it. Your business and cash can simply flow if you abide in truth and stand your ground unsentimentally.

The Queen of Coins has the necessary experience. We see this from her position, turned not towards the one making an offering, but rather turned towards the void. That is her confidence, namely, that she can afford to stare into the void. She holds her own coin up in a gesture that makes us think that she's ready to add to the three above her.

If you have experience, you don't need to worry about what happens when your working power is exchanged for pleasure. You will work because you love it. The last conversation here between the Knight of Batons and the Queen of Cups testifies to that.

I can't help but laugh a little at the middle column: The Magician knows how to move mountains, how to make the swordsman act in accordance with his will or magical power.

Running a business IS knowing the power of magic, knowing the power of the samurai, the power of fairness, the power of the coin and the sword forged in fire, and the power of love.

The best business strategy is this: To do what you love and to abide in justice.

Abiding in truth is not about emotional narratives, melodrama and vulnerable stories that sell. It's not about boosting 'big me', impaling 'small me', or flattering 'important you.' It's about flow, the flow of nothingness whence moving mountains is not even a big deal, but something that you do every time as a matter of course, effortlessly and completely fearlessly.

As for nuance, you can ask yourself this: A sword for three coins; a cup for a baton... What's the difference?

Incidentally, it's not for nothing that Justice presides over the Queen of Cups, whom gravity pulls towards where trustworthiness is concerned. You CAN cut somebody into halves as an act of kindness...

Insofar as this tableau begins with the Queen of Swords, who is traditionally associated with the opposite of trust, and ends with the Queen of Cups, who is associated with benevolence, we can further argue that what makes your business strategy successful is your ability to tell a believable story that inspires.

But there's a catch.

You may have a clear a vision of your goals, a cutting-edge focus, and strong determination, but if you don't know how persistence works **with** change, not against it, then you don't know the value of your own story.

By saying NO to conmen, you say YES to the discerning factor.

You can KNOW what a Magician does, and use his shape-shifting ability to your own ends, but you can also KNOW that you can do better, when you combine showmanship with absolute faith in the fact that, ultimately, life flows and it happens exactly as it happens, quite independently of what you make of it.

The believable story is, after all, a mirror you hold up to others. Meanwhile, what you can do for yourself is exercise the art of kindness, in love and war alike.

Wait for It

When we say, 'I'm out of time,' we don't always refer to being unable to complete a task according to schedule. 'I'm out of time' can also refer to a sense of escaping time.

Being out of time in this sense means being beyond change. But being beyond change does not mean being beyond expectation.

As you cannot experience being out of time in the sense of being out of it, as in, being beyond consciousness, or dead, you cannot escape having some sort of expectation. After all, experience generates more experience, not a reconciliation of opposites.

The interesting thing about waiting is that when you do it, you can at the same time witness how your experience of what you expect generates more experience of what you can both live and imagine at the same time.

Just think: The more you wait for something that's anticipated by your senses, the more your adrenaline gets you out of yourself in the sense of placing you besides yourself.

If prolonged, this act of waiting for your senses to realize themselves through mundane channels of manifestation turns into nostalgia of various degrees, ranging from romantic feeling and melancholia to obsessive pathology. Note that the senses are NOT your emotions about them.

If you want to know what I'm talking about, beyond taking this as a point of academic discussion, then bring to your mind a time when you were in love. When you're in love you're out of time.

We don't love with our emotions, as most people think. We love with the heart. Quite literally, when're we're in love we experience waiting for the lover with a lot of blood pumping through our hearts. This is not an emotional response to love, but rather very much a somatic one.

The same applies to eating a dish that makes you swoon, or to listening to a piece of music that transposes you somewhere that's quite unbelievable. There's a whole science on waves carrying out sound vibrations to places that usually connect you to a piece of memory, smell, touch, or other sensorial impressions.

It is for this reason that we can consider waiting for something with all our senses one of the most poetical acts; also because when things go wrong, it's not because of the senses, but because of the emotions that mess up the senses. It can be pretty disastrous to remember the taste of vinegar as something sweet.

But just think: In the context of reading cards for love questions, how many times have you come across this very situation, when a woman, for instance, remembers her abusive relationship as something soothing and comforting, thereby being ready to continue in her imagination to entertain the idea and hope that her lost 'lover' will someday return to her.

There's a lot of anxiety in the world. Part of it has to do with how we register and archive our sensorial impressions, and the fact that we end up waiting for the wrong thing. The other part relates to the fact that most have lost the ability to wait altogether.

Even popular sayings that used to be associated with virtue are now considered fatalistic: 'All good things happen to those who wait' is now a phrase that many scoff at, forgetting that the implication of this saying is far more interesting than the reason for its dismissal, one that has to do with prioritizing action over inaction.

Waiting is also an act, of course. To forget that means to forget what action really is, namely, the process of doing something. The process of doing something is not 'success', as many fallaciously believe, but rather, performing a deed.

When you just wait, and don't think about it, thus distorting your waiting with memories of stories that can turn more and more colorful, what you do is place yourself beyond time. In this sense the saying, 'all good things happen to those who wait', expresses waiting beyond change, which is time's corollary.

When your waiting bypasses your memory, you find that it acquires the quality of symbolic and non-verbal communication. Linguistic competence, eloquence, and analysis turn into a kind of poetry that is the manifestation of what's closest to your senses when they express themselves. In other words, you find that when your waiting is poetic, and therefore symbolic as it's not tied with your verbal language of desire, you can easily wait even for that which you lack the words to say or for that which you think you need time to unfold.

Now some would ask: If you can't be explicit about what you want, how can you develop any strategies of waiting for it?

This is a good question, and the answer is that you can't. But when we talk about forms of mysticism and personal gnosis, then we're with the possibility of knowing things beyond the words.

Such knowing is usually the result of first struggling with ambiguity (poetic language is always ambiguous), and then with exorcising scepticism out if its limits (logical language is always about that).

While waiting beyond the words that can articulate what you're waiting for is always a transgressive act, it has a very pragmatic function, namely, that of knocking off all your illusions about your emotions and how exactly they relate to the realm of the senses.

Speaking on the mundane level, you can, for instance, have the sense that you're done with the work you're doing now. You can even observe how your body rejects that work, with your kidneys and bladder not being able to regulate the piss anymore. You ignore this subtle message because you're emotional about changing lanes. After all, you've invested more than 25 years in your career. You go to the doctor's for a remedy, while entertaining the illusion that if only you can keep going, you'll enjoy success.

But what if there's another alternative? If you're tired of being on time, of being on beat, and of the call 'action, action, action' that completely disregards all your senses, then you may want to ask your cards this question:

How can I get better at waiting? How can I place myself out of conventional time, so that when I eat, I eat, when I sleep, I sleep, when I make love, I make love, without at the same time investing myself in other, side narratives than the simple ones I'm already engaged in sensually creating?

Before you lay down any cards, think of the following:

If you get pip cards and court cards, think of them as connectors to your ability to wait with all your senses whether this waiting is for something clearly defined, or for something that transgresses the normative codes.

Don't think in cliché divisions, à la cups are for love, or coins are business. If you ever read erotica literature, or watched a French film from the 60s on the play of gazes, then you'll know how much love a piercing sword can possess, or how sublime a musical orchestration your baton can inflict on your ears.

A quick look at the question posed here based on a reading of three cards can disclose the following:

5 Cups, King of Cups, 8 Batons

No matter how self-indulgent it may appear, the best way to wait for something to unfold naturally is through distancing yourself from making any rigid identifications with the thing you're waiting for.

Two cards here emphasize two different stages of flow:

One is dynamic: 4 cups get together to celebrate the 1 in the middle. The other is static: we take note of the decorated cup in the hands of a King.

Clearly there's a rhyming scheme here to remark, as we connect the cup in the middle of the 5 Cups card with the one in the King of Cups card.

The flow that has two natures can create this story:

The King says the following to a gathering of grossly intertwined sticks:

'This cup here, it's special. You can't have it. Not only that but I'm the one who helped it turn into a thing of beauty, thus separating itself from the others.'

What I find enticing here is the gesture of the King:

Free hand on hip, and legs turned towards the cards of the more immediate senses, the ones that have flow embedded into their nature. He acknowledges the pressure from the batons: 'You got a special cup, what are you going to do with it, what is its purpose'?

This King is clueless. The King of Cups is not into those kind of disciplining calculations. He is an aesthete. Dionysus of the senses, not of structural planning. If anything, he IS the very representative of the suit of pleasure.

The message that we can take from this is clear:

You can get good at waiting, at focusing on just the one 'special' thing that you hold in your hand, by completely disregarding the blocks building up in front of you.

From the perspective of flow, where is there any space for the consideration of obstacles? What obstacles? Such questions are indeed most transgressive.

§

More generally if we want to wax more than poetic, we can consider this philosophy:

A cartomantic reading session with the full deck goes through **four stages** of recognizing what's happening:

Intensity, arousal of curiosity (though this can also have sexual content), **nonsense and silence, and repetition.**

On this list I particularly like the last two: When the reader establishes intensity through reference to basic curiosity, 'nonsense' takes over and articulates itself forcefully, yet paradoxically, through silence.

There's always a moment in the reading session when both the reader and the sitter can be baffled, so they 'say' nothing. Because silence is instituted, there is thus a need for the repetition of all the other movements. This repetition is what constitutes transgression.

While this transgression often comes close to being interpreted as a form of obsession – the reader is obsessed with decoding, and the sitter is obsessed with the urgency to know things – it also ensures that something interesting happens between the reader spinning off a story that the sitter brings to the table and the sitter whose story is often one of secrets.

The brilliant insight is that because transgression is what it is, a site of struggle and tension with language and ideas, it cannot *per se* also be the vehicle for communication as a result of precise readings (across and between the agents involved).

In other words, everybody misreads everybody else – but not entirely. That's the beauty of cartomancy.

A reader may estimate a sitter's response quite accurately, but not because she is able to read her opponent with infallible precision – via classical cold reading or through the plain clarity of the cards – but because there is always a chance that she is wrong precisely and inasmuch as she is also right.

I like this idea, especially as it relates to an ethical question: How much responsibility does the reader of cards have to show to their sitters? Here the correct answer must be this one: None.

Not a single nerve of responsibility must be shown, if waiting for the good thing to happen is to stand a chance of survival in its intense, ravishing, illuminating, and for the most part violent mode – violent in the sense that such a waiting act violates the most basic cultural expectation, which is to wait for dictations from above to know what is appropriate and what is not, instead of just knowing due to seeing things as they are, and as they unfold in the ever-mysterious NOW.

Tarot cards are **sensorial triggers.** The trumps make us aware of the order of things, and they give us a blueprint for how we can transgress such orders. The pip cards and the courts connect us to modalities of transgressing our inherent limits of being in the world.

You see the Ace of Spades.

Now ask yourself without thinking of standard meanings: How many times was your sense of this card similar to this decision: 'That's it. Up until here, and no more?'

Here some would ask: 'Wait, isn't that the job of the 10 Swords, to make us realize that we've had it?'

I would suggest that by the time we got to the 10 after the initial, ultimate decision was made, what we would actually say is this:

'I did it. I have fully realized the big NO. I'm now connected to the full stops of my life.'

The Decisive Factor

Most people who have been following my cartomancy writings over the years have learnt that my least favorite card in the tarot pack is the Lovers.

I keep coming back to this card, and almost always have bashing things to say about what it does in relation to the card it happens to be in play with.

The big baton below says: 'It's here. Take it.' But does our Lover hear that? He never hears a thing; he never sees a thing; he never does a thing. You'd think a big offer like this would energize our anemic. It doesn't.

The standard meaning of this card is associated with love or choice. This is what I don't like about it already: Regardless of what we say or mean about it, the card itself seems not to be able to make up its mind as to what it wants to represent beyond configuring forms of ambivalence.

Most people get excited, however, when the Lovers are in the picture. I get it, as this excitement ties in with the reason why we bother to reads cards at all: We read cards because we want guidance for our choices.

Cards can show us alternatives: They indicate how we measure up in the game of comparing to others, they point to which way to go, they give us strong impressions of what we really like and what we really don't like. In other words, almost every reading session with the cards is all about what the decisive factor is when we need to make a choice. It's no wonder we get excited.

The Lovers shows up in your reading. Excellent. Now what? This card has the least potential to solve your problems. If auspicious at all, it tells you that you've reached a level of confrontation – some are in denial about that. How well do you know yourself? If you have to make a choice, is it based on knowing your mind, or is it based on hearsay, listening to the opinions of others?

The answer to this lies in looking at what other cards, trumps and pips alike, you find nearby. As the Lovers will never give you clarity on what the decisive factor is when you find yourself at a crossroads, you need to figure out what you know about the value of things.

A decisive factor simply means possessing knowledge of a specific property. Lacking this knowledge leads to indecision, to more ambivalence. When you get this card, you get a signal that you need a resolve.

Let's look at an example.

You have a marriage proposal, or one that invites you to share your life with another. You know it in your heart that if you follow through, it will be a good thing. But you're not sure about what goes into making it stick. After all, so many divorce already three months after.

If you were to know what they all thought on their wedding day, you'd find that many would say this: 'I did it because I knew it in my heart that this was the one.' But as things change all the time, and as history has also diligently been recording, the heart tends to possess a different kind of knowledge, taking place quite often immediately after the wedding night.

So what makes it stick?

If you posed this question from the outset, you'd find that what you need is not to ask your heart about it, but rather, to know what your decisive factor is.

Many would swear that what makes a relationship last is the intertwining of three essential properties: both parties have solid mental stability, both parties can provide solutions to problems that arise, and both parties can laugh together.

If you wanted your decision to be influenced by something more tangible than what the heart has to say, especially when it's in cliché mode, then you'd take your knowledge of such specific properties into account. Mental stability, ingenuity, and humor are often a safe bet. Others prefer passion, endurance, and honor.

Have you ever thought of why the Lovers card features three figures on it, other than to tell us explicitly that here we're with an indecisive situation, with the young man in the middle hesitatingly asking himself: 'This woman to the left, or that one to the right'?

Formally speaking we're here with a triangle, three variables that can lead to the determination of three winning factors that you can bet on – keep in mind though that as there's never any guarantee for anything in life, what you do when you make a decision is never anything other than forecasting.

Ideally any choice is based on seeing both the explicit and implicit underlying structure of a matter. The explicit gives you focus. The implicit gives you perspective. Focus creates a sense of distinction; wide perception enhances play. This is enough already to keep you excited.

But how do you avoid mixing up the levels? How do you know what your heart knows, either explicitly or implicitly, and which one is when?

I actually experience this very situation in my practice of reading cards that's a problem: People often present implicitly a predicament whose premise ought to be recognized as explicit, and vice versa. Many a time I want to ask them: Can you please make up your mind about it? What do you really want to know?

In strategies of decision-making this is bad. What can we do, then, to sharpen our vision as to what our decisive factor is when the premise for what we want to know is not always clear?

A useful practice is to read a string of cards for the situation, and then select from your string the one card that you think is a 'problem' card, the one that necessitates knowledge of your decisive factor.

This is standard practice if you mainly use the trumps in your readings, only making recourse to the pip cards if you need clarification. Some call this following 'the French school.'

The Lovers card is a usual suspect that often calls for the pip cards to 'clarify' it, but any other trump, pip card or court card can also pose a similar, challenging situation, and hence call for more pips on the table.

With this 'problem' card in mind, what you can do is reshuffle your deck and do another reading with view to learning something about your trifecta, your winning order of the specific properties that speak in favour of your making a clear choice.

Let me give an example based on a recent experience that has choice in focus.

As a lover of the samurai culture, aesthetics, and philosophy, there's no end to my love of the samurai sword. So I do the rounds in the antique collectors' world and educate myself as to which blade is the best that I can invest in according to what I can afford at a certain moment in time.

One such blade was suddenly within my reach, and then out of my reach again due to inattention. I was vacationing with my family over the holidays and I got distracted.

While thinking about returning to the sword in the middle of the family circus, my superego also started censoring my desire with this question: 'What is the purpose of this'?

I gave in, even though I already know that there isn't any purpose to anything whatsoever, and that in effect there's nothing I ever need, not even food. I missed the boat on the purposless thing. The collector took the sword off the market quite suddenly.

The best part, however, is that this event gave me an opportunity to entertain myself. First, I observed my behavior around my reaction, ranging in emotion from 'oh no, this is what I get for my ambivalence,' to 'let's engage in a game of prediction and see what happened.'

While the first manifested as regret, the latter manifested as joy in reading the cards about it. I even shared the story in the social media on Instagram – where's the fun in predicting if you have no witnesses? I formulated this question in three parts:

Did the Danish collector take his samurai sword off the market because: 1) I hesitated to put down $10.000 for it? 2) He sold it to another? 3) He regretted the decision to sell his precious possession?

Three cards fell on the table, and they had this to say:

'The collector was negotiating an offer, but the sword didn't change its status quo. He still has it.'

Phew, I felt much better.

I love social media. People expressed their sympathy on this, along with their good wishes for another occasion.

As I wanted some validation for my story and implicit prediction, I kept watching the collector's space. Meanwhile, I also had an occasion to practice the high art of Zen patience. My waiting time was rewarded.

Two weeks later, the sword was back on the market. The cards were correct on two out of the three points that I could verify:

The *katana* was still with the collector, and the price was unchanged. If we assume that an offer was made, as the cards suggested judging by the presence of the eager Knight of Batons, now we can see that collector didn't take it.

My blood pumped through my heart very fast: 'Oh, such a fine Hizen blade from 1650... I'm not going to let it go again.'

With the conditions changed towards favouring a second chance, I can say the following: While the heart was resolved in what it wanted beyond ambivalence, what was still missing was the decisive factor.

What are the three specific properties that can speak in favour of making this investment?

One is scarcity and rarity. The second is the reasonable price that reflects the value of the sword. The third is indulging my youthful folly and not underestimating the power of useless things forming a collection.

But what do the cards say? What is my decisive factor in buying the samurai sword according to the cards?

Let's have a look at this personal reading, as it poses a few interesting aspects:

First, let us bear in mind that this question is also a setup, as it challenges me to recognize the possibility that whatever I also recognize as specific properties that can influence me in my decision can also align with saying no, rather than yes to it.

A decisive factor can pull you in both directions, one where you go with it, and another where you go against it.

Second, note also that when I ask the question about what my decisive factor is in this given situation, I'm not merely asking a question led by modality, such as, 'why should I do this', as the answer can easily be one-sided: 'Because I want to.'

Possessing knowledge about the specific property of something is not the same as giving in to whims. In my desire and concern here, I want to know more about my motivation.

If I picked up where I left off, namely from my sense of relief at seeing Temperance signifying that the sword is still in the possession of the collector, we can now investigate into what this may suggest.

In and of itself Temperance is associated with the virtue of moderation and regulation of flow. You're neither too excited, nor too indifferent.

With this in mind, let's pose the question again:

What is my decisive factor?

Queen of Cups, 4 Coins, King of Batons

Here I laughed on two counts: First, while shuffling, the Queen of Cups fell out of the deck 4 times, before I laid down the cards. Second, I laughed because every time the queen landed on the floor, I'd pick it up and put it back in the deck with this very thought in mind: 'Because you want to.'

I guess I insisted on putting it back in the deck because I didn't want the situation of 'because you want to' for no other reason. It goes to show: My poor ego has very little chance of winning over the power of my unconscious desire.

When this is said, let's see.

The decisive factor here **is** 'because I want to'. I may as well admit this as one of the specific properties that makes this sword worth the while.

What I get to pay is not a lot. The 4 Coins card testifies to making a stable investment in line with what I can reasonably afford. The value of such swords is also a classic. People create value through the stories that they believe in. This has hardly ever to do with the thing itself. I'm not even sure one can put a price on a fine piece of steel made by a first or second-generation family of sword-smiths from the 1600s.

The man who sells the sword, the King of Batons, is not as sharp as the King of Swords. Perhaps he doesn't quite know what he's got there, though inveterate collectors tend to possess specific information. Where collectors are a bit 'special' is in their being consistently higher when it comes to the value of their collection. The interesting thing here is that neither the Queen nor the King look at the money involved. Which is not a lot, again, all things considered. Why is that? What are they looking at instead?

Two more cards fell on the table, the Lovers and the Moon.

The Queen is looking at the Lovers. Why am I not surprised? Here's our usual suspect, the initial ambivalence that started this whole story. In this light the Queen says, 'I'm not quite sure about this, but I still like it, monetary value or not.'

The King is looking at the Moon. Is he mad to sell his sword at this relatively low price, or is he merely confused about it?

I leave it to you to determine what you think my decisive factor pulled me towards.

§

The overall point here is that what we can take from readings with the full deck is the following:

Whereas the trump cards describe a situation ever so explicitly, the subtler pip cards, featuring an arrangement of geometrical patterns that are not immediately intelligible to the eye, give us insight into the decisive factors that can go into influencing the situation at hand.

The court cards are the go-betweens, mediating between choice and decision-making, situations and their conditioning, polarities and the stretch of tension between extremes, and so on.

We're still with the basic cut here, with the pip cards exhibiting their power by virtue of their connecting us to the way in which we understand the metaphors we live by.

The ultimate question that the pip cards invite us to consider is always this one: How far do we stretch it, and for how long before the elastic bursts? How sharp is your decisive factor?

Burning Bridges

'Don't burn all your bridges,' they say, without always thinking that before we burn any bridges there has to be a crossing of them first.

How many do that? How many actually cross bridges before they burn them?

How many cross bridges and then commit to this resolve: 'Not only have I crossed the bridge, but I also burned it. And it was good'?

Bridges connect one thing to another. They are liminal spaces. Sometimes, however, these liminal spaces must be pulverized in order for something new to emerge.

Burning bridges is not always about regret. Quite the contrary. Sometimes they spell this out: There's only one path: To move forward, to keep going.

You can make recourse to past memories, as it's not easy to vanquish them whether they are good ones or bad, but you can also think of them in a detached way, in a way that's completely devoid of personal involvement.

Why? Because whichever way you turn it, by default the only path is the way forward.

The past does nothing for you. You can entertain yourself with analyzing 'what happened' and then with 'what happened afterwards', but you can also remember that identifying with what happened, or clinging to what happened as a way of honouring your memory, leads to exactly nowhere. There's no virtue in honouring victimhood.

The good news about all connectors is that what is being brought forward in the combination of what is ahead of you with what is behind you has precisely the quality of forwardness.

There's only one path: Moving forward. Defying flow, resisting, or turning back is a disgrace to your breath, to your potential to build bridges of your own.

So far we've explored how the pip cards act as connectors, before they happen to mean anything. Take this example of a reversed victim story based on these cards:

Queen of Batons, Ace of Batons, Force, Queen of Spades

Little Red Riding Hood has an important task of delivery. Suddenly on her path she meets the big bad wolf. She takes out her blade hidden in her wooden scabbard that looks like a baton, and deals with it.

End of story.

You can imagine who won. I think I see some hairs on the ground...

Meanwhile, the Ace of Batons here doesn't mean 'new projects'. It simply acts as an adverb: Suddenly...

Think: Batons are fast. The first is surprising. Ten of them are just tiresome already.

The Queen of Batons's baton rhymes with the Queen of Swords's sword. Vitality turns into resoluteness: 'Either I win, or the wolf does. I prefer it that I win.'

End of story.

Storytelling with cards is not a new invention, though sometimes you can come across ideas that present it as a new invention. Same thing with the obvious realization that what we do with the cards is create narratives that follow a particular sentence structure.

'Oh, so the cards can be about something else than inner psychology and personal gnosis?'

'Yes,' some answer in earnest to the question devoid of pretence, while others will hurry to take advantage of the situation and present sentence-making as the new holy cow in town.

There are bridges and bridges. Some are built across new and old wisdom, some are built across selfish interests. If you happen to realize that you've crossed the latter, burn it. [1]

Then keep going.

Look at how things are connected in your practice of reading the cards. It's not about learning a 'new' method. It's about connecting the cards to a place that has to do with your ability to know context, to know what story you're in, and to know what place you have in the story.

You are never 'just a reader of cards.'

Sometimes you're Little Red Riding Hood, cutting right through it with her new samurai sword.

---

1 For excellent studies in storytelling with the cards, consult the works of fiction writer Italo Calvino and Tarot reader and philosopher Enrique Enriquez.

Free Will

Much of my teaching revolves around insisting on the signifi-
cance of making preliminary assessments before any reading of
the cards takes place. This includes looking at HOW people for-
mulate what they put on your table.

One of the most essential things that I do is always take that into
account, as it gives me insight into what precisely it is that people
cling to. If you practice enough, you'll see common themes and
patterns emerging.

Most people who consult a fortuneteller cling to the illusion of
control, making recourse to that other big illusion called 'free
will'. Compensating for what most perceive is a lack of control,
you'll get to hear a lot of stories of guilt and victimhood.

Determining the degree of intensity of such stories can be a good
idea. If the cards are already on the table, you can check with the
elastic again: How stretched is it? The batons are a good indica-
tor of this. How snappy? You're with the swords here. How lax?
Welcome to the cups. How shiny and embellished? Here is the
story of the coins.

Sometimes I deliver this kind of message:

'There's nothing you can do about it'.

I'm looking at these cards:

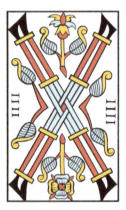

8 Swords, 4 Batons, Hanged Man

The other is appalled. 'What do you mean? Surely your cards must point to the ways in which I can grow and transform...'

The voice gets more and more desperate, which just happens to confirm my suspicion of the fact that here I am again with a story about a desired identity, self-empowerment, and control, before an acknowledgment of what the situation is already exists. How can you transform anything as long as you're in denial about what is?

'There's nothing you can do about it,' I insist. On occasion the other also insists, while slamming the door in my face, and walking out triumphantly: 'I have free will.'

I stick to my guns. I read the cards I get. If the other wants to talk about free will disguised as a desire to control, I cut her short and don't budge at all to accommodate her fantasy of transformation.

We always do the things we do, quite independently of what we think is the personal, original, and creative clichés we like to serve ourselves. There's no such thing as 'authentic free-will self'.

Life happens as it does, and the reality is that only what's under your nose counts. You can check the veracity of this if you ask yourself this question: 'Am I reading these words because I decided to get this book, or am I reading these words simply because I happen to read them right here and right now?'

What's under your nose is not for you to change, but for you to humbly observe and get on with the program in accordance.

There's lots of liberating power in this stance, as it relieves you of the thought that you have to do things, do things differently, rise to expectations differently, thus wasting a lot of precious breath.

In my reading sessions, I thus look at what people cling to, and start my readings from there. There's also a lot of discarding too: Not this, not that, and not this other thing either. I go for the bare bones.

In terms of action, if I give advice towards transformation, I look at this question too, as part of the preliminary process: What condition is this person I'm reading the cards for subjected to? I don't fall for urgency: 'Hells bells, tomorrow is Monday and you're so going to change this shit, you have free will.'

What is the certainty I'd speak with if I said that? Where would it come from? From seeing the future? From granting that we all have free will? From pointing to transformative mojo we can be lucky to have been born with?

While I'll advise the person to act upon her free will on Monday, will she be able to see how life passes under her nose right now, without her making any effort? If I can't point to that, and make the other understand the exact implications of that, then I will do nothing other than participate in continuing her fears.

If I were to boil all this down to one essence, I'd say the following: The reason why there CANNOT be any free will is because NOW trumps it.

In our illusions to decide, change, even change perspective, transform, and whatever else we have in this register, what we actually do is live according to circumstance and condition. We don't change anything, but circumstance and condition can change for us.

Free will presupposes consideration of the past, as in 'I won't do this anymore as it's been bad for me,' with view to getting a better future, 'tomorrow I'll change tracks and will feel much better.'

This is where I put people on the spot, people I read the cards for. I simply ask them, 'are the past and the future real?', when they insist that their cards give them something to compensate for what the cards on the table already show they are in denial about.

When the cards suggest to people: 'Get real', they are not even kidding. Neither the past nor the future is real, so here's the million-dollar question in relation to temporality that we can all pose to ourselves:

What would we exercise your free will against, when we eliminate the past and the future from the equation, an elimination that's necessary simply because both the past and the future are fictions, memories, or wishful thinking?

There cannot be any free will because NOW always trumps it, leaving us no other option than to live life as life happens. The sooner we realize this, the more we get to live a life free of worry, arrogance, and personal impetus.

It is in this observance of how life happens as it happens that we can locate the universal power of the pip cards as it connects us to the biggest trump ever, the NOW that encompasses the functions and duties we that we happen to fulfil in life:

> Now I rule, now I race for success, now I retreat, now I slash throats, now I give, now I judge, now I hang, now I dream, now I love, now I AM.

The pips tell us how all these functions and duties are performed, and with what degree of energy or apathy, of stretching it or not, how fast or slow. Some dice are best rolled with a cold head. Some books are best read with a hot heart.

Let's end here with a meta-wish. Here's an example of a meta-wish: 'My wish is that all my wishes come true.'

In some stories there's prohibition against meta-wishes, as they have a tendency to crash the system.[1] But let's pretend we don't know that.

Now let's ask the cards:

I wish I had free will, how can I get it?

The implicit meta-wish here is this: if you have free will, then we can assume that everying you want you'll get.

2 Cups, Queen of Coins, 8 Coins

The cards, drawn entirely at random in a game with witnesses, say the following:

---

1 See *Gödel, Escher, Bach: An Eternal Golden Braid* by Douglas Hofstadter (1999)

There's dualism in the world, one that makes us feel good, like a good wine in our cups transposing us to a place of comparison: 'My cup is half full, yours is half empty.'

You must exchange this feel-good duality with one idea. What passes through your empty mirror?

Many things align with what you see, like soldiers in some golden armor, and you can participate in this command: 'If you can think it, it exists.'

You CAN think 'free will', and so it will exist.

But is it real?

Beyond Cards and Magic

In addition to this book here, there's a deep dive into the power of the pips in the form of one recorded lecture followed by a live O&A session as part of the series of talks BEYOND CARDS AND MAGIC.

The Power of the Trumps: A Subtle Burst

is also available as a pack of eight video lectures, a recording of the live Q&A session that took place after the release of the lectures, and a pdf version of the book.

Visit
Aradia Academy
aradiaacademy.com

§

BEYOND CARDS AND MAGIC
is about reading quirky, complex, tried and tested texts and grimoires, and whole cartomantic systems through the lens of the Tarot cards.

BEYOND CARDS AND MAGIC
opens a gate to the possibility to read with the cards against the grain, bust a few towers, and laugh.

Lightning Source UK Ltd.
Milton Keynes UK
UKHW02f0339020218

317205UK00009B/134/P